ROBERT XAVIER RODRÍGUEZ

GAMBITS
SIX CHESS PIECES
for Horn (or Bass Trombone/Tuba) and Piano

(score and parts)

ISBN 978-0-6340-0314-7

G. SCHIRMER, Inc.

DISTRIBUTED BY

HAL•LEONARD®
7777 W. BLUEMOUND RD. P.O. BOX 13819 MILWAUKEE, WI 53213

www.musicsalesclassical.com
www.halleonard.com

PROGRAM NOTE

Gambits, Six Chess Pieces for Horn and Piano was commissioned by Charles and Sarah Riehm and completed in October, 2000. It is dedicated to Andrew Riehm and the *Musica Nova* ensemble of the University of Texas at Dallas. Motifs from the game of chess unite the music and titles of the six movements, as follows:

I. In the aggressive opening fanfare, "White vs. Black" (marked *Andante bellicoso*), the piano plays only white keys while the horn plays pitches corresponding to the black keys of the piano, alternating stopped and open pitches. At the end, the piano quietly "captures" some of the black keys, whereupon the horn immediately wins by taking possession of the white tonic note (C) with a triumphant rip (*glissando*).

II. The title, "Giuoco Piano" (Quiet Game"), refers to the chess opening of that name. A simple *cantilena* in the horn flows over a gently rippling piano sequence.

III. "Muy Ruy" pays homage to the sixteenth-century Spanish chess master who created the most popular of all chess openings, named in his honor, the *Ruy Lopez*. The music, accordingly, is a Spanish *fandango*, with variations of increasing intensity in the horn over a driving piano ostinato.

IV. The slow introduction of "French Defense" is built on a French sixth chord in the piano answered by small intervals in the horn, corresponding to the small pawn moves which characterize the French defense in chess. An expansive *allegretto* follows, in the style of a Parisian cabaret song.

V. "Sicilian Defense" is built on the traditional Baroque 6/8 *Siciliana* dance rhythm.

VI. "Copa Capablanca" celebrates the Cuban chess master, José Raoul Capablanca. The music is cast in the Afro-Cuban rhumba form, with alternating syncopated strains in major and minor. The work ends with brilliant horn *glissandi*, as in the opening movement.

Robert Xavier Rodríguez

duration ca. 12 minutes

for Andrew Riehm

GAMBITS
Six Chess Pieces for Horn and Piano
I. White vs. Black

Robert Xavier Rodríguez

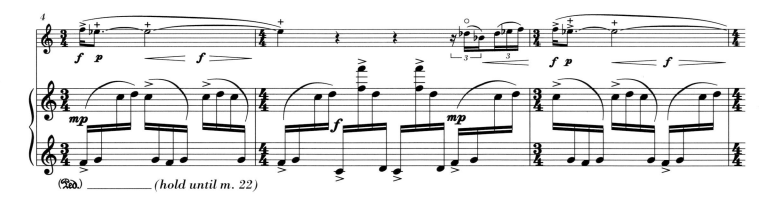

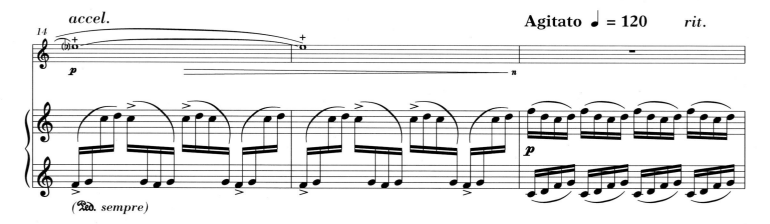

4

Andante ♩ = 92

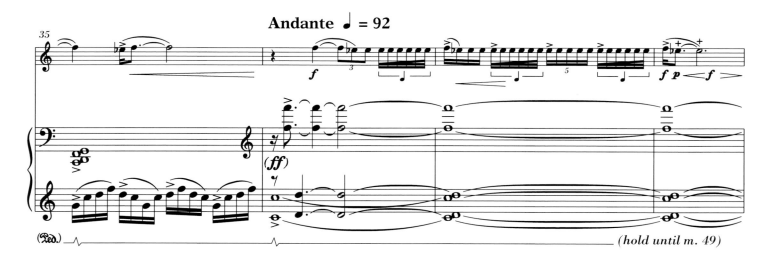

(hold until m. 49)

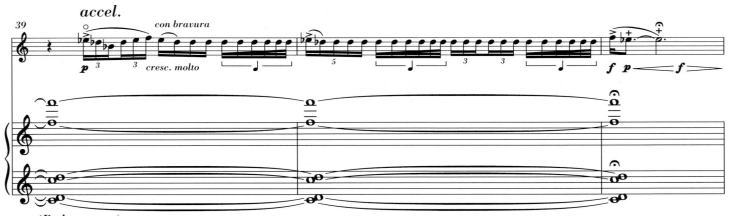

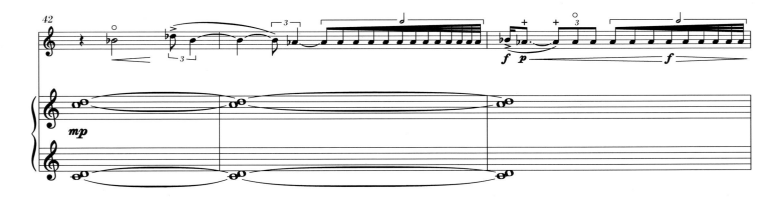

6

II. Gioco Piano

Allegretto grazioso ♩ = 120

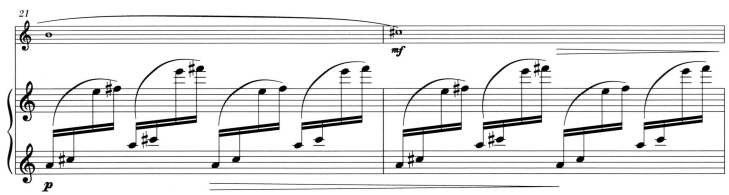

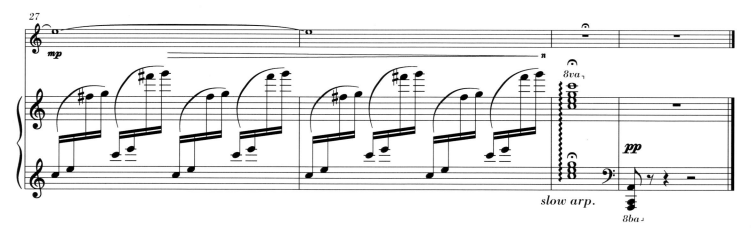

III. Muy Ruy

Tempo di fandango (prestissimo) ♩ = 160

Horn in F

for Andrew Riehm

GAMBITS
Six Chess Pieces for Horn and Piano

I. White vs. Black

Robert Xavier Rodríguez

2

II. Gioco Piano

III. Muy Ruy

IV. French Defense

4

V. Sicilian Defense

Tempo di siciliano (larghetto) ♩. = 50

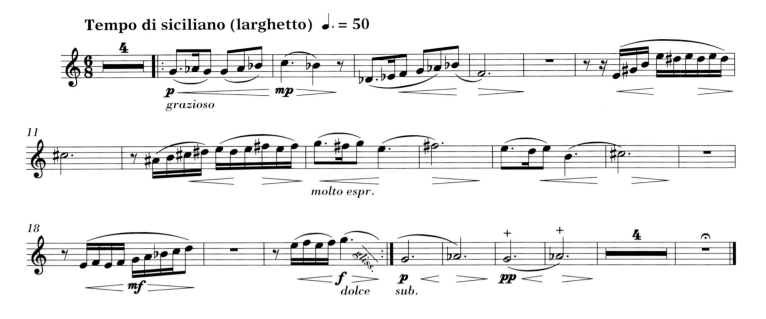

VI. Copa Capablanca

Tempo di rhumba (presto furioso) ♩ = 152

for Lyndsey Hoh

GAMBITS
Six Chess Pieces for Horn and Piano

I. White vs. Black

Bass Trombone *or* Tuba

Robert Xavier Rodríguez

2

II. Gioco Piano

Allegretto grazioso ♩ = 120

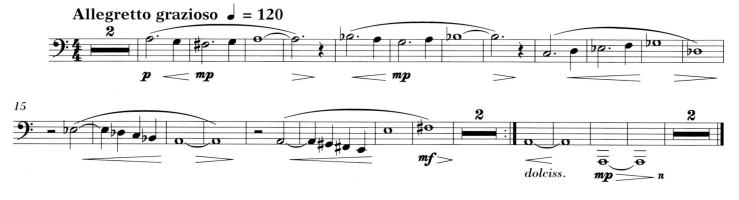

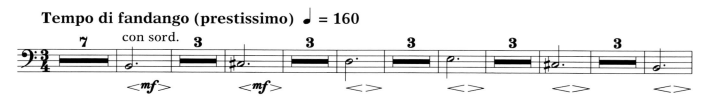

III. Muy Ruy

Tempo di fandango (prestissimo) ♩ = 160

107

114

121

126

IV. French Defense

Adagietto ♩ = 80

Allegretto parigiano ♩ = 120

13

legato espressivo sempre con licenza

22
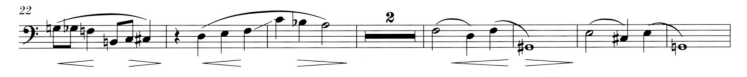

poco   a tempo
rit.

31

39

V. Sicilian Defense

Tempo di siciliano (larghetto) ♩. = 50

VI. Copa Capablanca

Tempo di rhumba (presto furioso) ♩ = 152

IV. French Defense

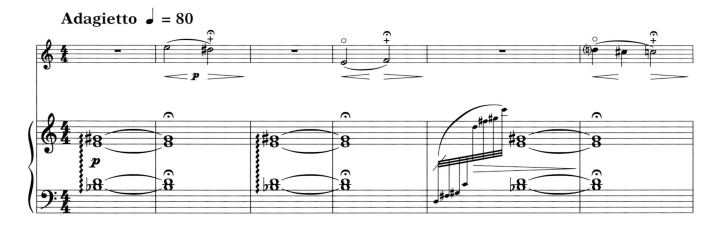

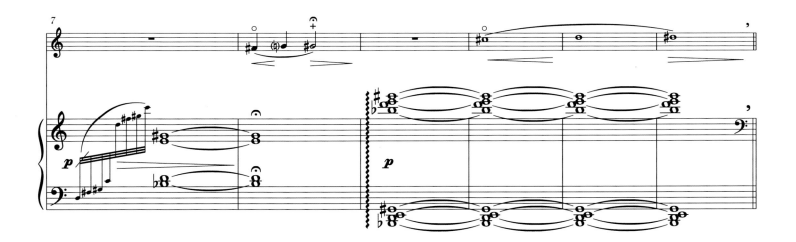

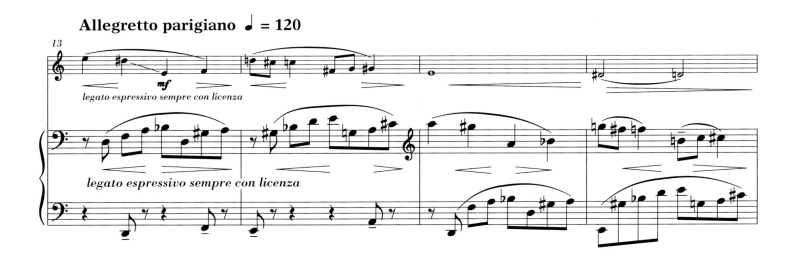

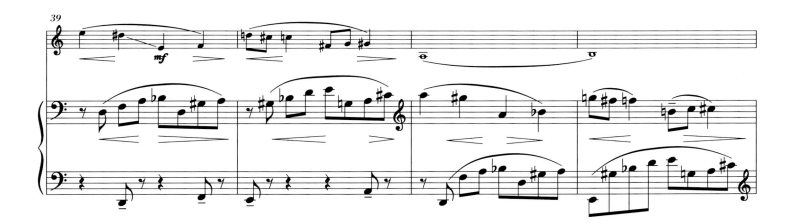

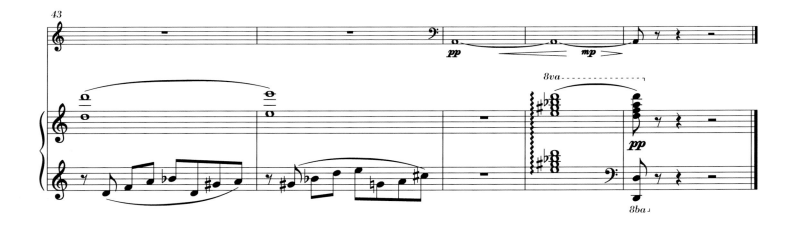

V. Sicilian Defense

Tempo di siciliano (larghetto) ♩. = 50

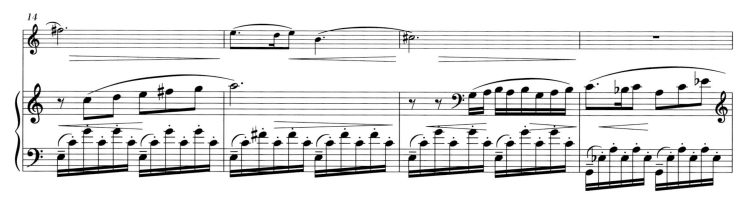

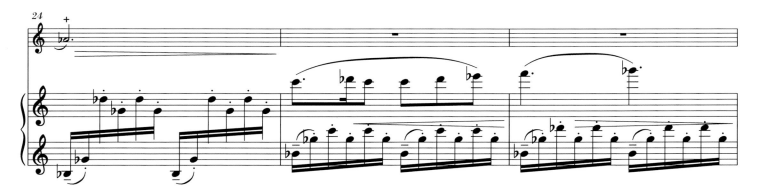

VI. Copa Capablanca

Tempo di rhumba (presto furioso) ♩ = 152

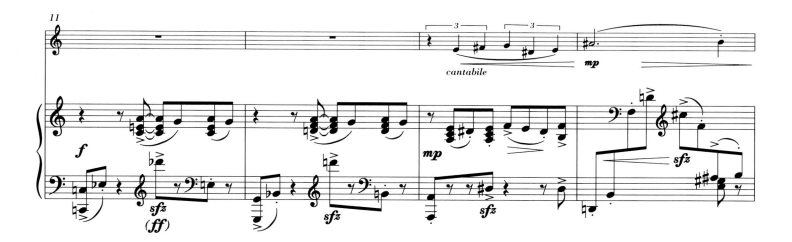

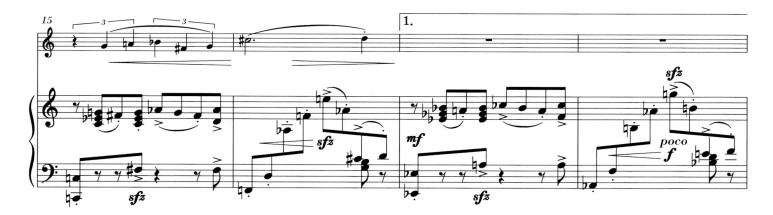

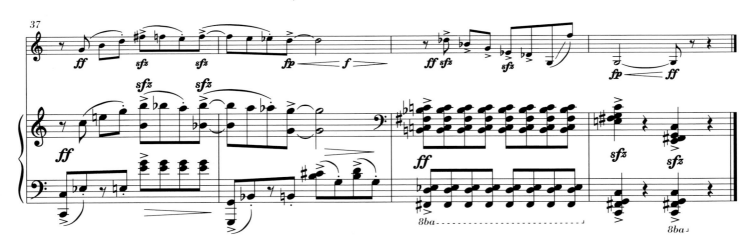